Language Varies

Hi Reader,

My name is Nandi. I am a linguist. Linguists like to learn about how people communicate.

I love that people communicate in different ways. This is called *variation*.

Some people think variation is bad or wrong. Linguists, like me, know variation happens because everyone is unique! We think variation is exciting, interesting, and important!

You might communicate like the people in this book. You might not communicate like the people in this book. That is okay!

The way you communicate is awesome.

~ Dr. Nandi Sims

By Dr. Nandi Sims

Rourke

BEFORE AND DURING READING ACTIVITIES

Before Reading: *Building Background Knowledge and Vocabulary*

Building background knowledge can help children process new information and build upon what they already know. Before reading a book, it is important to tap into what children already know about the topic. This will help them develop their vocabulary and increase their reading comprehension.

Questions and Activities to Build Background Knowledge:

1. Look at the front cover of the book and read the title. What do you think this book will be about?
2. What do you already know about this topic?
3. Take a book walk and skim the pages. Look at the table of contents, photographs, captions, and bold words. Did these text features give you any information or predictions about what you will read in this book?

Vocabulary: *Vocabulary Is Key to Reading Comprehension*

Use the following directions to prompt a conversation about each word:
- Read the vocabulary words.
- What comes to mind when you see each word?
- What do you think each word means?

Vocabulary Words:
- *alike*
- *dialect*
- *styles*
- *vary*

During Reading: *Reading for Meaning and Understanding*

To achieve deep comprehension of a book, children are encouraged to use close reading strategies. During reading, it is important to have children stop and make connections. These connections result in deeper analysis and understanding of a book.

Close Reading a Text

During reading, have children stop and talk about the following:
- Any confusing parts
- Any unknown words
- Text to text, text to self, text to world connections
- The main idea in each chapter or heading

Encourage children to use context clues to determine the meaning of any unknown words. These strategies will help children learn to analyze the text more thoroughly as they read.

When you are finished reading this book, turn to the last page for an **After-Reading** activity.

Table of Contents

English Varies

Ana is my new friend. I speak differently than Ana. Ana speaks differently than me.

4

English can **vary**. No one speaks the same.

5

People sometimes use different words for the same thing.

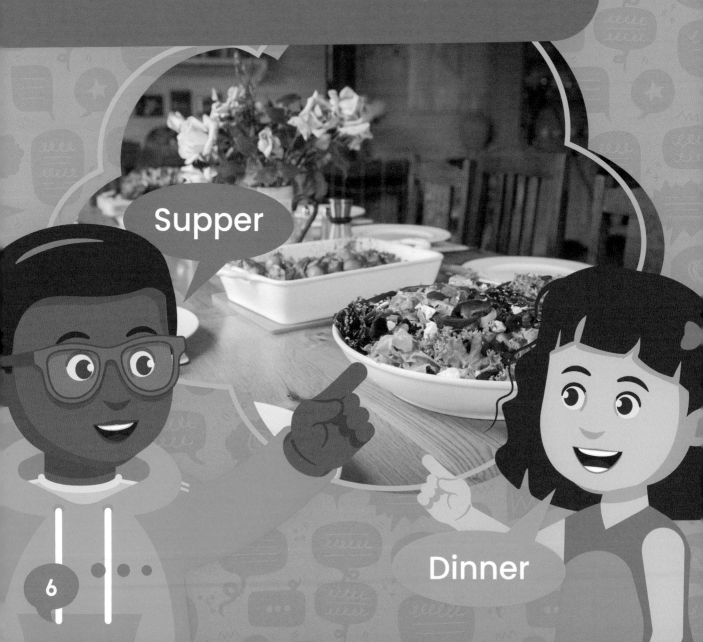

Supper

Dinner

Ana calls this a *cart*.
I call it a *buggy*.

What do you call it?

7

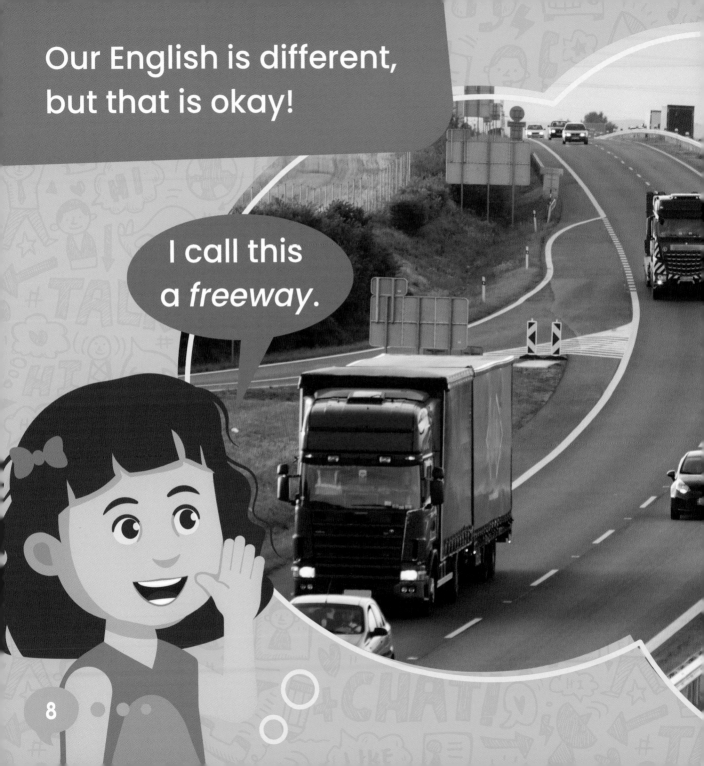

Our English is different, but that is okay!

I call this a *freeway*.

8

People Vary

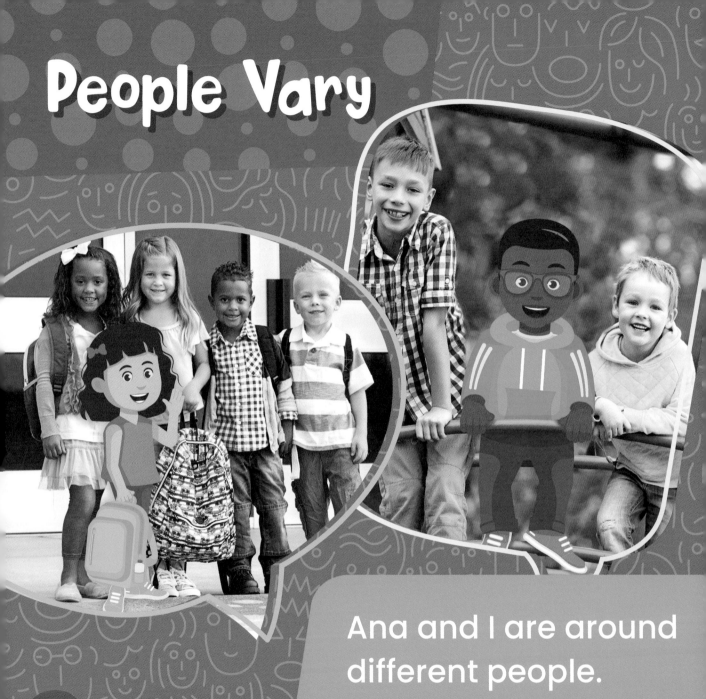

Ana and I are around different people.

I know words that she doesn't know.
She knows words that I don't know.

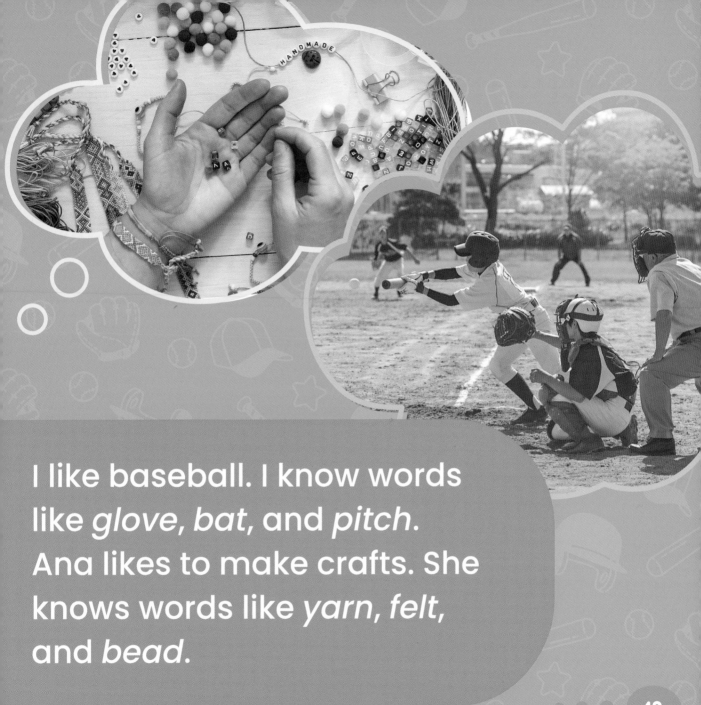

I like baseball. I know words like *glove*, *bat*, and *pitch*. Ana likes to make crafts. She knows words like *yarn*, *felt*, and *bead*.

Regions Vary

North Central

Northern

Western

Midland

Ana is from California.
She speaks a western **dialect**.

I am from Virginia. I speak a southern dialect.

Northern New England

Southern

Find your state. What dialect do you speak?

15

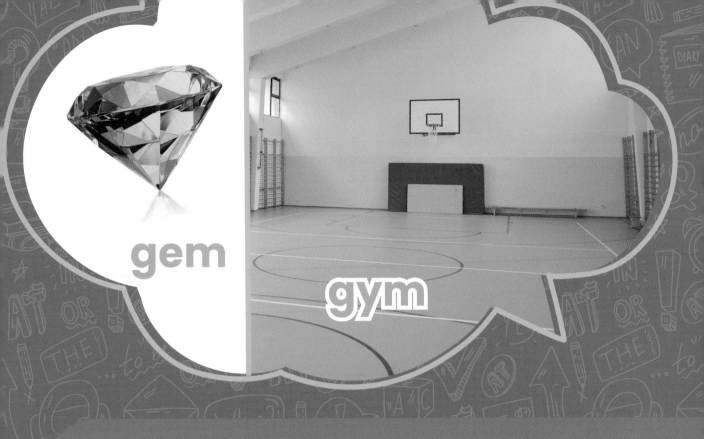

gem

gym

They do not sound alike when Ana says them.

Our words sound different because we are from different places.

Settings Vary

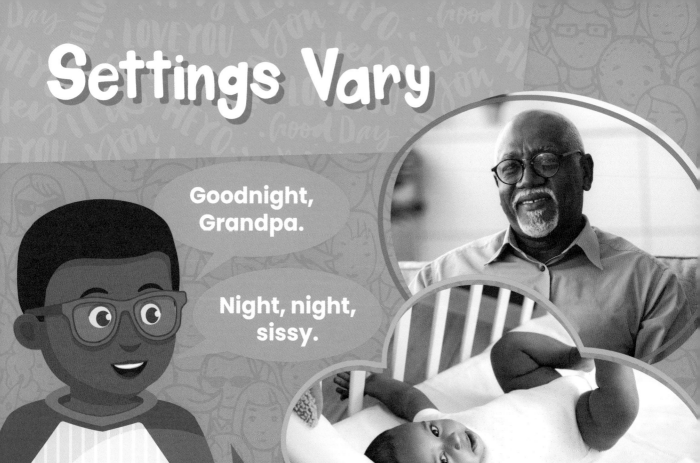

Goodnight, Grandpa.

Night, night, sissy.

The way I talk to my grandpa is not the same way I talk to my baby sister. I can use many **styles**.

The way Ana talks to our teacher is not the same way she talks to her friend. She can use many styles.

We both speak English, but we don't speak the same.

Photo Glossary

alike (uh-LIKE): in a similar way

dialect (DYE-uh-lekt): a way a language is spoken in a particular place

styles (STILEZ): the way things are written, spoken, made, or done

vary (VAIR-ee): to change or to be different from something similar

Activity: "What Is This?"

Linguists often do research by asking people about the words they use. Now it's your turn to do some research.

Supplies

crayons, paper, pencil

Directions

1. Create a table like the one below on your paper.

2. Find a few friends. Point to each picture you drew and ask them what they call that object.

3. Write down their words in the right column.

Does everyone use the same word for each object?

Object	Common Words for Objects
	• _____ • _____ • _____
	• _____ • _____ • _____
	• _____ • _____ • _____

Index

About the Author

Nandi Sims earned her PhD in Linguistics from The Ohio State University. She loves to research language variation in communities. When she is not researching, teaching, or writing, she is often dancing or walking one of her five dogs.

After-Reading Activity

One way to learn new words is through a hobby. With an adult, do an online search about a hobby that you want to learn about. Make a list of words about the hobby. Next to each word, write down its meaning and draw a picture to show its meaning.

Library of Congress PCN Data

Language Varies / Dr. Nandi Sims
(Words in My World)
ISBN 978-1-73165-275-1 (hard cover)(alk. paper)
ISBN 978-1-73165-245-4 (soft cover)
ISBN 978-1-73165-305-5 (e-book)
ISBN 978-1-73165-335-2 (e-pub)
Library of Congress Control Number: 2021952202

Rourke Educational Media
Printed in the United States of America
01-2412211937

Edited by: Catherine Malaski
Cover design by: Tammy Ortner
Interior design by: Tammy Ortner
Photo Credits: Cover, p 1 © Fer Gregory, © Andrew Angelov, © Monkey Business Images, © Dr. Nandi Sims, p 4-5, p 22 © BearFotos, © saravutpics, p 6 © Photos BrianScantlebury, p 7 © Pressmaster, p 8-9 © TTstudio, p 10 © Brocreative, © Olesia Bilkei, p 11© Photographee.eu, © mTaira, p 12 © Africa Studio, p 13 © Dudzenich, © mTaira, p 14-15, p 22 © pingebat, p 16, p 22 © Mega Pixel, © AlenKadr, © Designs Stock, p 17 © Retouch man, © ESB Professional, p 18 © Prostock-studio, © Pixel-Shot, p 19, p 22 © GK1982, © ElenaYakimova, p 23 © sorayut, © Evgeny Karandaev, © Petr Jilek, p 24 © Dr. Nandi Sims